175th ANNIVERSARY

1834 - 2009

175

Facts About Marietta

Rebecca Nash Paden

Joe McTyre

Original Art by
Barbara Betts King

ACKNOWLEDGEMENTS

Published Sources:

Scott, Thomas Allan. *Cobb County, Georgia and the Origins of the Suburban South,* Marietta: Cobb Landmarks and Historical Society, Inc., 2003.

Temple, Sarah Blackwell Gober. *The First Hundred Years—A Short History of Cobb County in Georgia,* Marietta: Cobb Landmarks and Historical Society, Inc., 1989.

Yates, Bowling C. *Historic Highlights in Cobb County,* Marietta: Cobb Landmarks and Historical Society, Inc., 2001.

Millard, Janet M. *A Woman's Place: 52 Women of Cobb County, Georgia 1850-1981,* Marietta: Cobb-Marietta Girls Club, 1981.

Lassiter, Patrice Shelton, *Generations of Black Life in Kennesaw and Marietta, Georgia,* Charleston, S. C.: Arcadia Publishing, 1999.

Elgin, Peggie R., *Centennial Celebration,* Marietta: Marietta Schools Foundation, 1992.

Providing assistance to the authors:

Marietta Welcome Center Executive Director Theresa Jenkins; Gone With the Wind Museum Director Connie Sutherland; Marietta Daily Journal Bill Kinney, Otis Brumby Jr., Joe Kirby; Cobb County Public Library, Georgia Room Director Carolyn M. Crawford; Marietta Museum of History Director Dan Cox; Atlanta History Center, Mike Brubaker; Marietta High School Principal Leigh Colburn, Pat Shields, Dwight Smith; Lockheed Martin, Damien A. Guarnieri.

City of Marietta: Mayor Bill Dunaway, City Manager Bill Bruton, Assistant to the City Manager Shannon Barrett, Tammy McCommon, Suzanne Johnson; Ward 7 Councilman Philip Goldstein, Planning Department Director Rusty Roth, Norma Higgins, Shelby Little, City Clerk Stephanie Guy, Yvonne Williams, Shirley Thompson, Marietta Housing Authority Director Ray Buday and staff, Public Information Officer Matthew Daily, Jason Bourne, Parks and Recreation Director Rich Buss, Police Chief Dan Flynn, Fire Chief Danny R. Rackley, Marietta Power and Water General Manager Bobby Lewis, Lori Swafford, Public Works Director Dan Conn.

Cobb County: Commission Chairman Sam Olens, Communications Director Robert Quigley, Craig Ford; Christy Roselle, Earl Smith Strand Theater.

Louis Walker, Deane Bonner, Michael Hitt, Pam Billingsley, Laura Harding, Sara Nichols, Adrian Pressley, William R. Paden, John Nash, James W. Nash, Dempsey Kirk, James W. Corley, Linda Bricker.

All photos, unless credited below, are from the collection of Joe McTyre.

Among other photo collections are those from the following sources: Bob Basford, Randy Weiner, Marietta Museum of History, Dr. James L. Skinner III, Marietta High School, Harpers Weekly, Charles M. Brown, James B. Glover V, Robert M. Goodman, Sara Nichols, Louis Walker, Marietta Gone With The Wind Museum, Cobb Landmarks and Historical Society, William R. Paden, Charles C. Clay, Robert B. Ormsby, Sally Litchfield, Johnny Fulmer, Guy H. Northcutt Jr.

Other photographs by Johnny Walker Photography, Becky Paden, Erin Parr, William Penninger, Thinh Nguyen.

Authors Note: The various usages of the words "colored," "blacks," and "African-Americans" in this work reflect the time periods cited.

175 FACTS

INTRODUCTION

In the late 1820s, the land comprising present-day Marietta and Cobb County was inhabited by the Cherokee Indians. Drawn by the healthy climate, cheap, fertile land and an abundant water supply, scores of pioneer settlers soon arrived to claim the former Native American lands. By 1838, conflicts with the Indians led the Federal government to order the resettlement of the Cherokees in the western United States. With the advent of the railroad and the town's strategic location, Marietta became an important trading center.

Marietta has seen great prosperity but has experienced war, military occupation, reconstruction, depression and recovery in its 175 years. When designated the Cobb County seat of government in 1834, Marietta was originally bounded by Anderson and South Waddell streets on the southeast corner; Lemon and North Waddell streets on the northeast corner; Polk and Poplar streets on the northwest; and the point where Denmead and Anderson streets would later cross on the northeast. Today, the city's land area consists of 23.04 square miles and extends as far south as Windy Hill Road and as far north as Sandy Plains Road. To the northwest, the city limits stretch to Kennesaw Mountain National Battlefield Park and as far as the 120 Loop to the east.

This account is a chronological summary of the life and development of a thriving and still developing city---Marietta, Georgia, U.S.A.

1828

*The discovery of gold in north Georgia and the resulting demand for land ignited a confrontation between new white settlers and Native Americans.

*1830 Drawing by
Henry Merrell, courtesy Dr. James L. Skinner, III*

1829

*Newcomers to the area began pressuring the Federal government to force the Indians off their lands and give their lands to the white settlers.

1830 Drawing by Henry Merrell, courtesy Dr. James L. Skinner, III

1832

*Cobb County was established by the Georgia Legislature when the state divided the Cherokee Indian lands and parceled them to pioneers in a land lottery. In Cobb, 5,000 lots were drawn in the lottery.

Cherokee Indians and white residents met beneath the branches of the Treaty Tree to negotiate issues during the 1830s. The tree was located on the grounds of the Henry Greene Cole cottage on Washington Avenue, a marker for an area where the Indians left their weapons when they went into the town of Marietta. Lightning killed the tree in the early 1900s.

1833

*Pioneer settler James Anderson arrived in Marietta and built the first dwelling, a log structure on Church Street near the present site of St. James Church. Among others in the first wave of new residents included: Joseph Gault, the first lawyer to set up practice; Dr. Henry King, the town's first physician; William Root, the first pharmacist; John Lemon, the first Marietta merchant; David Irwin, Edward Denmead, William and Stephen Cole, Archibald Howell, William T. Winn and Ephraim Knight.

*The first church organized in the new settlement, Marietta Methodist Church, (now First United Methodist Church), held its first service.

*At the end of the year, Marietta had almost 100 residents.

1834

*Marietta was established as the Cobb County seat of government and incorporated as a village. The Legislature appointed James Anderson, George W. Cupp, Lemma Kirtley, Leonard Simpson and George Washington Winters to govern the town with authority to pass all ordinances and bylaws deemed necessary.

*The first courthouse was a one-room log building located southeast of the present day Glover Park's center. It was also used for worship services and other meetings.

1830 Drawing by Henry Merrell, courtesy Dr. James L. Skinner, III

*Among other early buildings, all crude log structures on dirt streets near the present town square, were two taverns, a drug store, a variety store and a worship building for all faiths.

*Two possibilities may account for Marietta's name. The town was probably named for the wife of Senator Thomas Willis Cobb, Cobb County's namesake. (The Cobbs never resided in Marietta.) Another notion is that Marietta is a combination of two names saluting two popular young ladies, Mary and Etta, who were among the first residents of the settlement. History records that the gentlemen were "dazzled" by the ladies' charms.

*In the early 1800s, Stagecoaches were a vital link to the outside world. In the North Georgia area, James R. Powell owned a thriving coach line linking towns from Kingston through Rome, then to Alabama. The stage provided mail delivery and an important means of travel until the railroad came with faster and cheaper transportation.

4

1835

*Baptist and Presbyterians organized churches in the new village. The congregations are now First Baptist Church and First Presbyterian Church. The first church built, probably by the Baptists, may have been erected near the present location of the Confederate Cemetery.

First Baptist Church

First Presbyterian Church

*The Marietta City Cemetery was established in the 1830s when the first known marked grave was prepared for eight-year-old William Capers G. Harris. Originally, the cemetery may have been the small burial ground of the first Baptist church organized in Marietta, built near the graveyard. Between 1848 to 1866, 19 slaves and freedmen were buried in unmarked graves. The Slave Lot at the cemetery is the only slave burial ground in any major Georgia cemetery.

1836

*Attorney and pioneer settler Joseph Gault began his law practice. Considered Marietta's first lawyer, he was instrumental in organizing the first inferior court in Cobb County.

1837

*The Methodists' first building was a log cabin similar to the replica erected in 2008 on the same site between Whitlock Avenue and Polk Street.

1838

*Federal soldiers rounded up Cherokees in Marietta and north Georgia and forced them to begin a 3,000-mile march (the "Trail of Tears") to Oklahoma.

*The second Cobb County courthouse was built on part of the Glover Park property. The building was a square white-painted two-story structure with a main floor courtroom and second-floor offices. It replaced the original log court building. The 1838 building was later moved to Washington Avenue, where it serves as a law office.

The porch has been added to this 1972 photo.

*William Root opened the first drug store in September. The next year he moved his business to the corner of Root Street and the square.

William Root

*Marietta's first postal service was established with James Anderson as the first postmaster. The first post office building was built in 1845 but no location is recorded other than the "south side of the square."

*Marietta adopted a seal to attach to official documents. The simple round image featured a sheaf of wheat and a sickle, indicating the prominence of agriculture in the area.

1839

*Charles James McDonald was elected Georgia's 19th governor. McDonald settled in Marietta in the 1840s. His service to Georgia continued as a Supreme Court justice from 1855 to 1859.

Charles James McDonald

1842

*St. James Episcopal Church was the fourth congregation organized in Marietta. Its first building was built in 1843 on the present site on Church Street. During the Civil War, Federal troops threw the church's new organ out onto the street but a church member salvaged it. The organ is still in use in the Lawrence Chapel.

1845

*The state-owned Western & Atlantic Railroad began running from Marthasville (now Atlanta) through Marietta. The line was completed through Cobb County the next year.

*John Heyward Glover built a breakfast house that became the Fletcher House hotel after later additions. Both Confederate and Union troops used the building as a hospital during battles around Marietta. When Federal soldiers burned the town in 1864, only the top fourth floor was destroyed. After the

Civil War, the hotel reopened under the Kennesaw House name.
*The city's population was 1,500.

1848

*Archibald Howell built one of the earliest Greek Revival houses on Kennesaw Avenue. The impressive Doric columns are among the largest in circumference in the state. Union General H. M. Judah, military adjutant during the Federal occupation of Marietta, chose the Howell House for his headquarters.

*Oakton Tannery was built by James Bolan Glover Sr. and John Wilder on Cassville Road, now Kennesaw Avenue, about 1870. It continued operating until the 1920s. The ruins are still visible.

1849

*Andrew Jackson Hansell, later Georgia's Civil War adjutant general, built Tranquilla, another of the city's grandest antebellum houses. While her husband was away leading Georgia troops,

Caroline Hansell held off a thieving mob with a small derringer.

1850

*Marietta was known as a thriving resort with three hotels, a park, impressive houses, natural springs, a mild climate and other attributes that attracted summer guests from coastal areas. Visitors were also drawn by the accessibility of the railroad and attractive accommodations.

*The business center included the square and the first block or two on streets leading from the square.

Anna and Milledge G. Whitlock are shown in front of their hotel, the Whitlock House, in the late 1800s The Whitlocks were known for their hospitality and operated the most popular stopping place for tourists in Marietta until fire destroyed the house.

1851

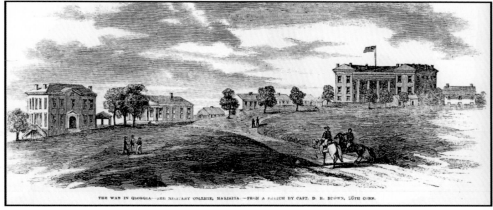

THE WAR IN GEORGIA—THE MILITARY COLLEGE, MARIETTA.—FROM A SKETCH BY CAPT. D. B. BROWN, 20TH CONN.

*Georgia Military Institute (GMI) opened, enrolling as many as 200 cadets who received training for military service along with scholastic instruction. The 110-acre campus with 17 buildings was located at the present site of the Hilton Atlanta/Marietta Hotel & Conference Center on Powder Springs Street.
*Marietta was one of the first towns in Georgia to have telegraph equipment installed.

1852

*Marietta was incorporated as a city, receiving its charter from the state legislature on January 22. The corporate city limits extended for three-fourths mile in every direction from the county courthouse in the square.

*John Heyward Glover was elected Marietta's first mayor.

John Heyward Glover

*Mayor John Heyward Glover donated the land in the heart of the new city for a park. Glover Park is one of Marietta's foremost attractions.

*The first town marshal was appointed by the city council. The law enforcement officer was the precursor to the police department organized later. In 1854 the voters elected the marshal but the council resumed responsibility for subsequent appointments in 1858.

1853

*Cobb County's third courthouse was built at the northeast corner of the square and Washington Avenue, facing west. The two-story Federal style brick structure stood until Union soldiers burned it 11 years later.

*Joshua Welch was elected mayor.

1854

*The town's first fire company was created by the Georgia Legislature on February 17, but no formal organization occurred until 1857. At least three devastating fires in the downtown area spurred its reorganization as Marietta Fire Company

Number 1 in 1857. Colonel J. W. Robertson served as the first foreman (chief). Soon afterwards, the city purchased the first fire engine and housed it in a brick building on Cherokee Street, headquarters of the Fire Company. A bell ordered for the fire engine arrived and went into use sounding the alarm. A parade was held around the square to mark the occasion.

*The Presbyterian Church was built on its present Church Street site. The original building is the oldest sanctuary still in use in Cobb County and was a Federal hospital during the occupation of Marietta in 1864.

*W. T. Winn was elected mayor.

1855

*I. N. Higgie was elected mayor.

1856

*Noel B. Knight was elected mayor.

1857

*J. W. Robertson was elected mayor.

1858

*R. W. Joyner was elected mayor.

1859

*I.N. Heggie was again elected mayor.

1860

*Samuel Lawrence was elected mayor and re-elected in 1861.
*Marietta's population was 2,667 including 1,175 slaves.

View of Marietta from the Alexander Street and Roswell Street area, probably about 1900.

1861

*After Georgia seceded from the Union on January 19, Marietta's population of 2,700 dwindled as men left in droves to join the Confederate army. Those unable to fight formed a home guard unit. Dozens of Georgia Military Institute cadets left school to join the fighting units.

1862

*The famous Andrews Raid (also known as "The Great Locomotive Chase") began in Marietta in April when a band of Union spies led by James Andrews spent a night at the Fletcher House hotel (later Kennesaw House) and boarded the northbound train the next day. Their mission was to capture the Confederate locomotive "General" and destroy the railroad tracks north of Marietta. While several members of the band escaped, most were captured, eight were executed and others were imprisoned or exchanged for Confederate prisoners. The 22 men involved were the first recipients of the Medal of Honor.

*J.A. Tolleson was elected mayor.

1863

*Townspeople continued to sacrifice to support southern soldiers by sending food, clothing, bandages and supplies to the army camps. The Confederates turned Marietta into a large depot filled with troops, wagons and rail cars carrying supplies for the Army.

* Jane Porter Glover donated a small parcel of land as a burial place for 20 Confederate soldiers who died in a train wreck north of Marietta. With the addition of two acres donated by Ann Moyer and lands acquired from the J. H. Glover estate, the Confederate Cemetery was established in 1867.

*W. T. Winn was again elected mayor.

1864

*In June and early July, some of the bloodiest fighting in the Atlanta Campaign raged near Marietta at Kennesaw Mountain, Cheatham Hill and Kolb's Farm. Marietta citizens cared for the Confederate wounded until the army moved south toward Atlanta. Union General William T. Sherman and his troops paraded through Marietta as they occupied the town and the GMI campus on July 3. Sherman's headquarters was set up briefly at the Fletcher House hotel. The Presbyterian Church, the Bostwick-Fraser House, hotels and other buildings were requisitioned by the Federals for use as hospitals. Citizens were confined to the town under martial law. Some who remained helped care for the Union wounded.

GENERAL SHERMAN'S ADVANCE—VIEW OF THE PUBLIC SQUARE, MARIETTA, GEORGIA.—Sketched by Theodore R. Davis.—[See next Page.]

*In November, departing Federal soldiers stole valuables and edibles before setting fire to the county jail, which was destroyed along with the Courthouse, at least 100 buildings and the railroad tracks. The three surviving downtown buildings were three floors of the Fletcher House, Denmead's warehouse and the Masonic building on the square.

*Federal authorities suspected Confederate nurse Fanny Fraser of spying for the southerners. No evidence was found, however, and she continued working throughout the Civil War. Fanny came with her mother Ann Couper Fraser to Marietta from St. Simons Island in the 1850s. Fanny's sister, Rebecca, was accused by Federal officials of spying for the South but they released her after she convinced them of her innocence.

*Church bells were given to the Confederate government to be converted into ammunition during the war. The fire department bell was used at St. James Episcopal Church, then returned to the engine at the end of the war.

*When the Sanges family prepared to flee before the Federal troops' invasion, the family matriarch refused to join her family in a boxcar on the last train leaving town. She insisted the cow must go too so the family loaded the animal into one end of the car while Mrs. Sanges and other family members huddled around the sofa at the other end during the trip to Madison. After the war, the cow again joined the family on the trip back to Marietta.

15

*Union General William T. Sherman ordered 400 Roswell women and children factory workers to march 16 miles to Marietta where they were loaded onto cattle cars and shipped north to Indiana and other places. A few made their way back after the war but most never returned. (Roswell was part of Cobb County until 1932).

*H. M. Hammett was elected mayor.

1865

*Marietta soldiers returned home to a very different place after the South surrendered in April. Marietta, once a lovely peaceful town, was mostly a blackened ruin. At least 100 houses and businesses were destroyed or badly damaged. Food was in desperately short supply.

The Third Cobb County Courthouse stands in ruins after Sherman's Union troops passed through.

*Once order was established after the devastation, C. C. Winn was elected mayor and served until October 1 when he resigned. A. N. Simpson was elected to fill the remainder of the term.

1866

*While most townspeople and returning Confederate soldiers were without jobs, some fortunate residents found work constructing a new Federal cemetery on Washington Avenue. Marietta resident Henry Greene Cole, a Union

sympathizer and accused spy, donated the 26-acre site. The Marietta National Cemetery is the burial place of 10,000 Federal soldiers from the battles nearby. Almost 8,800 graves of other veterans of every subsequent war are laid out on the quiet hill overlooking the city. The cemetery features a distinctive masonry archway built in 1882-1883 with 35-foot high Doric columns and ornate iron gates. The military cemetery is listed on the National Register of Historic Places.

*Robert M. Goodman established the Marietta Journal, the first newspaper in Georgia printed on newsprint manufactured at a paper-making plant in its own county. Eight years after it was founded, W.S.N. Neal and J.A. Massey purchased the Journal from Goodman. In 1909, the first merger of the Journal and another newspaper was made, resulting in the Marietta Journal and Courier. The long-time weekly newspaper became a daily in 1935. Otis A. Brumby Sr. merged the weekly Cobb County Times with the Marietta Daily Journal in 1951. Otis A. Brumby Jr. joined the company in 1965 and was named publisher in 1967. Soon afterwards, the newspaper began a major expansion project, publishing community newspapers to serve the Atlanta suburbs.

*A. N. Simpson was elected to a two-year term as mayor.

*On April 8, Zion Baptist Church organized the first black congregation in Marietta. Charter members were 89 former slaves who previously joined the Baptist Church with white members. The new Zion congregation built a frame building on land donated by the Baptists at the Lemon and Haynes Streets intersection. The church met there until its new brick building was completed in 1888. Zion has built two additional houses of worship, the latest a 1,160-seat sanctuary at Cherokee and Lemon streets.

1867

*DuPre's, Marietta's oldest downtown merchant, opened for business as Anderson Brothers. In 1927, H. N. DuPre bought the building, a cotton warehouse at the time, and changed the business' name to DuPre's. The store later sold garden and farm supplies, appliances and lighting and is now an antique store.
*The Federal military authority withdrew from Marietta.

1869

*Property and business owners began making improvements on the battered town square. Sidewalks were constructed, new shade trees were planted in the park, and, the next year, a new fence around the park replaced the one destroyed during the war.

*The city of Marietta's financial report stated "a very satisfactory condition of city finances. Not a dollar of indebtedness for 1869." But the Cobb County treasury had a total of 16 cents in its coffers the same year.

*G.W. Cleland was elected mayor. He served two years.

1870

*William H. Tucker was elected mayor. He served three years.

*New businesses began moving to Marietta while some pre-war merchants rebuilt their stores.

*Denmead's Warehouse advertised French Brandy for sale in May.

1871

*Work began on a new jail after an improvement in the county's finances was reported.
*The town's first sewerage system was installed on streets around the square.

1872

*Reconstruction officially ended in Georgia, bringing some relief from the afflictions of war to Marietta. New stores advertised their wares in the Marietta Journal and the city reported encouraging financial signs.
*The county began construction of a new courthouse on the square.

1873

*In October, the first court session was held in the fourth Cobb County Courthouse on the Marietta square.
*The Brumby Chair Company developed from a cooperage business started by James R. Brumby soon after the Civil War. The chair manufacturer's best known product remains the Brumby Rocker.

1874

*Humphrey Reid was elected mayor for a one-year term.

1875

*William H. Tucker was again elected mayor.

1876

*Edward Denmead was elected mayor. He served two years.

1878
*Humphrey Reid was again elected mayor.

1879
*Gas lighting was installed in Glover Park.
*Some stores began selling ice cream a few times a week. Mrs. B. Schoenthal's store advertised "Bring your sweetheart around to try it."
*Joel T. Haley was elected mayor.

1870s – 1880s

*Horseback riding was a popular pasttime among Mariettans, along with horse-drawn wagons and dogcarts for outings, and bicycle riding became popular.
*The first bandstand was built in Glover Park. Concerts in the park were held on Monday nights while the new park fence and bandstand were brightly lit with candles.

1880
*Edward Denmead was elected to a four-year term as mayor.

1882
*Sarah Freeman Clarke opened the Franklin Lending Library at her Whitlock Avenue residence. When space prohibited continuing the library at her home, Miss Clarke raised $2,000 among her Boston friends to buy a lot for construction of a library building at the corner of Church and Polk streets.

Sarah Freeman Clarke

1884
*In March, Cobb Countians voted against continued liquor sales. At the time, Marietta had 13 saloons in its business section.
*Enoch Faw was elected mayor.

1885

*Marietta's business district included 20 grocery stores, four drug stores, five general merchandise stores, a furniture store, two variety stores and a jewelry store.

*W. M. Sessions was elected mayor.

1886

*Edward Denmead was elected mayor. He served two years.

Edward Denmead

*On January 4, the Marietta City Council authorized the erection of a tall pole in Glover Park, high enough to be seen from most of the houses in town. The pole was used for displaying weather signals, using information relayed by a network of observers. Different-colored stars and crescents were symbols for various conditions.

1887

*Harwood Seminary, a school for Marietta girls, opened in the Archibald Howell house, purchased by some of Marietta's leading citizens who were named trustees. In the late 1870s and 1880s, several small private schools had previously held classes.

1888

*Most of the buildings lost during the Civil War had been replaced at this point, 24 years after their destruction.

*One of the city's first banks was founded by R. W. Boone as the Marietta Bank. It later became the First National Bank of Marietta.

*Thomas W. Glover was elected mayor, serving until 1893.

Thomas W. Glover

1892

*Glover Machine Works, Marietta's first heavy industry, incorporated and began manufacturing steam locomotives. The business eventually produced more than 200 narrow gauge locomotives. In 1995 the Glover family closed the factory, located at the corner of Butler (now Atlanta) Street and South Cobb Drive, now the site of the Cobb County Water Department, and the company moved to Cordele.

*The Marietta Journal announced that "the first female ever on the streets of Marietta on a bicycle appeared on Saturday."

1893

*Construction of Marietta and Cobb County's first library was begun on Church Street. Sarah Freeman Clarke's dream of a Marietta library was fulfilled when the facility opened on October 26. The new building, named in her honor, was modeled on the great reading room of the British Museum.

1894

*The first black public elementary school opened with classes for students from first through seventh grades. Lemon Street was the site of the school. The new wood frame building housed about 500 students. The first principal was A. Tolliver.

* The Marietta Colored Elementary School was built on Lemon Street. The school lacked lights, adequate books and supplies.

*R. N. Holland was elected mayor and served until 1896.

*R.W. Moon was Marietta's first police chief, serving until August 5, 1895. Other law enforcement officials were called town marshals from 1854 to 1894.

*Marietta's first public school building was completed on the city's southeast side. White students attended classes there. Known for many years as Waterman Street School, the building was razed in the 1970s after the property was sold to the Salvation Army.

1895

*Crosby's Drug Store on North Park Square was the successor to Root's Drug Store, the first pharmacy in Marietta. Later, J. M. Hodges bought Crosby's and in 1943 William H. Dunaway purchased the business. The store remained on the square as Dunaway Drug Store until Bill Dunaway sold the Dunaway chain to Eckerds in 1989. When Eckerds closed the store in 1997, the square was without a drug store for the first time in 161 years.

*The Marietta Paper Manufacturing Company built Marietta's first waterworks, spurred by its need for large quantities of water for the industry. The facility was located on Rottenwood Creek on the present Life University campus site. Up to this time, private and public wells had been  the main source of water for the community. By the next year, the system pumped water to a 50-foot standpipe near Roswell Street. In April 1896, water was pumped into Marietta for the first time.

1896

*D. W. Blair was elected mayor.

D. W. Blair

*Alexander Stephens Clay was elected to the U.S. Senate where he served three terms. He previously served as a Marietta city councilman, state representative and state senator. He is the only citizen honored with a monument in Glover Park.

Alexander Stephens Clay

*Marietta's Board of Lights and Waterworks was created to own and administer water and electric utilities.

1897

*Marietta native Alice McClellan Birney cofounded the Parent Teacher Association (PTA), originally the National Congress of Mothers. She was recognized at the White House for her work and served as the organization's first president until 1902. Her girlhood home still stands on Kennesaw Avenue.

Alice McClellan Birney

1898

*Thomas M. Brumby Sr. was elected mayor for the 1898-1899 term but resigned before taking the oath of office.

*W.M. Sessions was elected mayor in a special election held January 8.

W.M. Sessions

1899

*Cobb County's fourth courthouse was remodeled. The clock tower was moved to the front corner. The columns and gable atop the portico were removed and the second story porch leading into the courtroom was enclosed with a brick wall.

1900

*Cotton prices rose steadily in the late 1800s and early 1900s, making the product the major money crop in the county. Farmers hauled their cotton bales to downtown Marietta to sell their harvest.

*The new century began with further recovery from the war's afflictions for Marietta and Cobb County residents.

*Marietta's population was about 4,500.

*The new Methodist Church, the congregation's third building, was built on Atlanta Street.

*John Bailey, a black man accused of attacking a white girl, was lynched on the Marietta square after a mob took him from the jail.

*Thomas M. Brumby Sr. was elected mayor for the second time.

1902

*Bolan Brumby attracted much attention when he took his wife Ida and children Lawrence and Bolan Jr. for a ride in his new Oldsmobile, one of the first motorcars in Marietta.

*Joe P. Legg was elected mayor.

1904

*John E. Mozley was elected mayor.

John E. Mozley

1905

*The Marietta Gem City Band played for President Theodore Roosevelt during his visit to Roswell, his mother's birthplace. The band played "Dixie" and "Home Sweet Home" when the president first appeared. Musicians struck up "My Country 'Tis of Thee" as Roosevelt made his way to the town square from Bulloch Hall, his mother's home.

*The Atlanta Interurban Railway commenced service with electric streetcars from Atlanta to Marietta. The service continued until 1947.

*Marietta was growing steadily, especially toward the north of town. The first subdivision construction began, including the extension of Church Street through the Freyer/Denmead property.

*Free mail delivery began in March. Postage rates were two cents per ounce until November 3, 1917.

1906

*One of Marietta's earliest industries was Gem City Bottleworks. The business was sold to Coca-Cola in 1910 and relocated to Husk Street.

.

*E. P. Dobbs was elected mayor. He served through 1909.

E. P. Dobbs

*The Marietta Board of Lights and Water, later to be named Marietta Power and Water, was established by city council to administer both water and electric utilities. Robert Boone, John Awtry and S. D. Rambo were appointed to eight-year terms as water commissioners. Fewer than 5,000 people lived in Marietta at the time. The bonds necessary to fund the start-up were defeated at the polls, but two years later $80,000 in bonds was approved for the project.

1908

*Citizens voted in November for bonds to finance the installation of a modern waterworks and sewerage system.

1909

*M. A. Mace Morris was named Marietta fire chief, becoming the first paid fire department head. He served until 1913.
*The first meeting of the Board of Lights and Waterworks was held May 31.

1910

*Marietta City Hall was located in a three-story building on Atlanta Street from 1927 to 1979. Built in 1910, the building was formerly the Masonic meeting hall. Before the building was purchased by the city, the mayor and city council held meetings in the Cobb County Courthouse. The building was demolished about 1980.
*Dr. S. D. Rambo was the first citizen to connect his home with the new waterworks. Quickly following were Joe Black, Judge Newt Morris and H. N. DuPre.
*E. H. Clay was elected mayor.

*A new Marietta post office building was completed on Atlanta Street and provided mail service to the community until 1963. Declared surplus by the federal government, the Cobb County-Marietta Public Library moved into the building and renovated some areas. The library outgrew the space and vacated the building in 1989. Now the structure is home to the Marietta-Cobb Museum of Art.
*The population reached 5,949.

1912

*In June, the city completed installation of an improved street lighting system, proudly referred to by citizens as "white-way lights." The Gem City Band played "Dixie" and the Marietta Journal described the lighting as "soft as moon beams and restful as music that brings sweet sleep from the blissful skies."
*J.J. Black was elected mayor.

1913

*Mary Phagan, a 13-year-old Atlanta factory employee, some of whose family resided in Marietta, was murdered on Memorial Day. She was buried in the Marietta City Cemetery. Factory Superintendent Leo Frank was tried and convicted of the tragic death.

Mary Phagan

*Haynes Street School opened (renamed Keith Grammar School in 1943). The school closed in 1970, and the building was razed.

1914

*The town was packed with people from all over the county on Saturday, April 25 when Alexander C. Beech flew his airplane over Marietta. Merchants contracted with Beech to fly over the business section to draw crowds to the downtown area. The first flight lasted only 15 minutes because of high winds. When the winds abated,

Beech and his airplane went up again and flew around the square at a height of about 2,000 feet, according to the Marietta Journal.

*E.P. Dobbs was elected mayor.

1915

*While Leo Frank was serving a life sentence for Mary Phagan's murder, a mob of men reportedly from Marietta hauled him out of a state prison and took him to Marietta, where they hanged him on a tree at the Frey farm near the present day Frey's Gin Road, close to Roswell Road. None of the mob was ever arrested.

Leo Frank

*Marietta Golf Club was organized in September. The club received a charter as Marietta Country Club the next year after purchasing almost 68 acres for $8,000 from Professor and Mrs. J. H. Smith. Smith and O.B. Keeler laid out a three-hole

course on the site. Morgan McNeel was the club's first president. Today the Marietta City Club golf course and the Hilton Atlanta/Marietta Hotel and Conference Center occupy the location.

1916

*James R. Brumby Jr. was elected mayor. He resigned in February 1922 after serving six years.

James R. Brumby Jr.

1917

*When the World War I military training camp was set up east of the city near Blackjack Mountain, citizens formed a Soldiers Welfare Committee to provide comfort for the off-duty soldiers.
*The intersection of Atlanta and Anderson streets was the scene of the first street paving in Marietta. A single brick mason, "Little Jim" Lucas, laid bricks at a rapid pace and, by the years end, the Atlanta Street paving was completed. Four years later, citizens

approved bonds for paving other principal streets.

1918

*Marietta citizens threw a party on April 5 for local soldiers deploying for service during World War I. The three regiments marched around the park and formed columns on three sides. Ceremonies included presentation of flags, music and refreshments.

*A worldwide influenza pandemic struck Marietta resulting in closing of schools, churches and movie theaters to prevent spreading the virus. Several men from nearby training camps died of flu and were buried in the National Cemetery.

*Leila H. Anderson and Virginia Gibbes Morris were the first women from Cobb County to serve overseas as army nurses.

1920

*Marietta's Clarke Library became a free public library in October.

*Marietta's population reached 6,190.

*The Marietta Women's Club was organized. Mrs. I. A. White was the first president.

1921

*Kennesaw Marble Company in Marietta, one of the largest marble finishing mills in the South, was destroyed by fire.

1922

*Gordon B. Gann took office as mayor on March 9. He served three years.

Gordon B. Gann

1924

*A Marietta High School building built on Winn Street at a cost of $645,500. The campus is now Marietta Middle School.

1925

*Ursula Jenkins led a drive to establish a high school for black students. She persuaded the Marietta school system to rent and restore an abandoned church on Harold Street. In 1925, the new school opened with 20 students in seventh and eighth grades. By 1929, the school added grades nine through eleven. Professor M.J. Woods became principal that year, expanding the curriculum and starting the first football team, band and PTA.

Ursula Jenkins

LATE 1920s

*Mattie Harris Lyon organized the Ladies Memorial Foundation and lobbied the state of Georgia to make improvements to the neglected Confederate Cemetery on Powder Springs Street. Mrs. Lyon, known for her charitable and civic work in the community, was president of the United Daughters of the Confederacy Kennesaw chapter and helped start the first Red Cross chapter in Marietta. The city erected a statue of the woman who took the lead in marking Confederate graves and restoring the cemetery.

1927

*The privately-owned Marietta Hospital on Cherokee Street was opened to serve the community.
*E. R. Hunt was elected to a term as mayor.
*Women's organizations in Marietta and Cobb County increased public interest in good roads and beautification of highways. "Pull Georgia Out of the Mud!" was resounding through the state with women's voices among the hue and cry.

1928
*Gordon B. Gann was again named mayor.
*Marietta Board of Education began receiving part of the city's income from water, lights and power charges.
*The first garden club in Marietta, the Flower Garden Club, was organized and is still active.

1930
*Thomas M. Brumby Jr. was elected mayor and served eight years until his death in August 1938.

Thomas M. Brumby Jr.

*The population was recorded as 7,638.

The Marietta city limit sign was located on South Atlanta Road across from the Economy Ice Cream Company.

*The Growers Market on Powder Springs Street and, later, other markets on the downtown square were often packed on Saturday mornings with farmers selling their agricultural products, chickens, eggs, sorghum, cider and numerous other homegrown items. The custom was a continuation of a tradition from the mid-1830s when the Cherokee Indians sold their baskets and venison among the cluster of early log buildings in the settlement.

*The city's first high school for black students, Lemon Street High School, opened. First named Marietta Industrial High School, then Perkinson High School and, finally, Lemon Street High School, the brick building contained four classrooms. The facility is now the school system's Performance Learning Center

1931-32
*A group of women representing several local churches operated a soup kitchen at St. James Episcopal Church, serving about 10,000 meals for hungry children and unemployed adults in a three-month period during the Depression. Mrs. Herbert E. Hague directed the project.

*After a referendum by voters, the city of Roswell renounced its 100-year long association with Cobb County to become part of Fulton County.

1933
*Marietta and Cobb residents celebrated their centennial in the midst of the Great Depression.

*Hazel Hodgson McNeel founded the Marietta Junior Welfare League to assist underprivileged children in Marietta.

1934

*Helen Catharine Griffin was the first woman elected as a tax receiver. Her election made her the first Georgia female to hold a political office.

1935

*Sarah Blackwell Gober Temple published "The First Hundred Years, A Short

History of Cobb County, in Georgia," written over a five-year period. A Marietta native, her 901-page account detailed Cobb County families, transportation, education, politics, social life agriculture, the Civil War and Reconstruction. The comprehensive work includes interviews of residents, research from old diaries and newspapers verifying the county's history.

Sarah Blackwell Gober Temple

*The art deco Strand Theater opened on September 24 with the premier of "Top Hat." The building was equipped with such "modern technologies" as heating and air conditioning, acoustical sound system, seating for 800 and a fireproof projection room. The first half of the lobby was originally an arcade with a kiosk ticket booth in the center. The Strand

underwent a complete renovation in 1964 with a large western mural hung in the lobby. Between 1982 and 2002, the building housed a variety of venues including a movie draft house, local rock bands, a church, an elections headquarters and a classical movie theater.

1937

*Continuing the city's annual Christmas scene begun a few years earlier, Marietta installed a large illuminated Christmas tree in the park.

1938

*The mayor and council created the Marietta Housing Authority (MHA) on May 9. T. C. Branson Jr. was elected chairman.

*In October, Paul A. Gregory was appointed by the board as the first MHA executive director at a salary of $250 per month.

*Voters approved a $10,000 bond program for city parks and a swimming pool.

*L.M. "Rip" Blair was elected mayor in September. He served until 1947.

*Virginia Gibbes Morris was the first public health nurse in Cobb County.

1939

*The Marietta Recreation Center Board was established in June, the beginning of the city's parks and recreation program.

*In the 1930s, glamorous actress and girlfriend of Chicago mobsters Virginia Hill visited her mother many times in Marietta. Her visits caused quite a stir and helped the town's economy as Virginia lavishly spent rolls of $100 bills.

Virginia Hill

1940s

*After much discussion between county and city officials, Larry Bell Auditorium was constructed on the 47-acre former county prison farm land at Fairground and Clay streets. (Clay Street is now the South 120 Loop.). The new building was designed as a recreation facility for Bell Aircraft Corporation workers and their families during World War II. The park's name honored the founder of the Bell Aircraft Corporation, operator of the new bomber plant in Marietta. Fire destroyed the auditorium in 1965. Eight years later, after proposed plans were almost scrapped because the low bid was almost $1 million over the original estimate, officials broke ground for the new $3.4 million Civic Center. A second building for theater and performing arts use was completed in November 1975. Besides the buildings, the park has tennis courts, a quarter-mile track, practice fields, a free play area, gymnastic center and an aquatic center.

1940

*After a federal report revealing that about 1,300 of almost 2,300 families lived in unsanitary as well as unsafe housing, Mayor L. M. Blair led the city council to pass an ordinance mandating indoor plumbing in all future Marietta houses.

*Clay Homes, Georgia's first low-rent housing project, was dedicated. The 312-

unit development located near the Marietta square was named for Marietta native and U.S. Senator Alexander Stephens Clay.

*Al Bishop was hired by city council at $80 per month to direct the new parks and recreation department.

Al Bishop

*Marietta had a population of 8,600.

*Marietta Mayor L. M. "Rip" Blair, County Attorney James V. Carmichael and other prominent citizens traveled to Washington to request construction of a new airport in Marietta. Their application to the Civil Aeronautics Administration (CAA) was aided by Major Lucius Clay, a Marietta native who ran the program.

1941

*The United States declared war on Germany and Japan. Marietta men were again called to military service and numbers of women also enlisted.

*The airport project proposed by Marietta citizens was approved and construction of Rickenbacker Field began in May. The Army Air Corps took over the airport in January 1942. It was renamed Dobbins Air Force Base in memory of Captain Charles M. Dobbins of Marietta whose plane was shot down in 1943, and also honored other Georgians lost in World War II.

James V. Carmichael   *Mayor L.M. "Rip" Blair*   *George McMillan*

1942

*On January 23, at a press conference held in attorney Jimmie Carmichael's office, it was announced that Marietta had been selected as the site for the new Bell Aircraft plant to produce B-29 bombers during World War II.

*Groundbreaking for the Bell Aircraft Plant in May 1942. L to R: Captain Eddie V. Rickenbacker, Jimmie Carmichael, L.M. "Rip" Bair and Cobb County Commissioner George McMillan.

*The first piece of steel driven for what was to become the main assembly, or B-1 building of the new Bell Aircraft plant, now Lockheed Martin.

1943

*Bell Aircraft Corporation completed a huge factory on the south side of the city and began manufacturing B29 bombers for use against the Japanese.

*More than 600 B-29 bombers were produced at Bell Aircraft.

*Women joined the ranks of Bell aircraft workers with "Rosie the Riveters" making up 37 percent of the wartime work force.

*Nancy Garner was Marietta's first female taxi driver, another non-traditional job women assumed during World War II.

*Marietta experienced a large population increase during World War II. The city had almost 18,000 residents, doubling the 1940 numbers.

1944

*The city council approved Lewis Park as the name of Marietta's first recreation area in memory of former Councilman John W. Lewis. The seven-acre park was donated to the city in 1910 as part of a larger tract designated for parks and waterworks. Lewis Park ranks as the oldest recreational park in Cobb County.

*Park Street Elementary School opened. Construction cost was $916,750. The school building is now the oldest in the Marietta City Schools System.

1945

*Germany and Japan surrendered to allied forces.

*Bell Aircraft closed its factory in Marietta.

*Pine Forest Elementary School was built on Aviation Road at a cost of $612,000. The building now houses the Marietta Center for Advanced Academics (MCAA).

1946

*Black residents of Marietta and Cobb County lined up around the courthouse and the county jail to register to vote after a court ruling declaring Georgia's 1946 all-white primary illegal.

*James V. "Jimmie" Carmichael won a plurality in the Georgia governor's race but lost the election because of the county-unit system in statewide races.

1947

*The electric streetcar stopped operating between Atlanta and Marietta in 1947. Marietta residents M. W. Kinney and Regina Rambo Benson were among passengers on the last run.

*Hattie Gaines Wilson helped initiate the first library for black citizens and served as the first librarian for the facility, located near the Child Care Center on Cole Street.

*Allgood Road and Dodd Street School buildings opened as day care centers for children of Bell Aircraft Plant workers. Both were converted to elementary schools for the 1951-1952 school year.

*Jimmie Carmichael became president of Atlanta-based Scripto, Inc.

1948

*Sam J. Welsch was elected mayor and served through 1955.

Sam J. Welsch

1949

*President Harry Truman presented the Distinguished Service Medal to Marietta native General Lucius Clay for his service as commander-in-chief, European command, and military governor of Germany from 1945 to 1949.

*General Clay was honored on Memorial Day by his hometown with a parade, speeches and barbecue on the town square. When the general's parade route passed the Atlanta Street house built about 1880 by his father, Alexander Stephens Clay, bystanders reportedly saw a figure they believed to be a ghost watching from a second floor window. Mariettans circulated a story that the general's mother, Sarah White Clay, watched as her son rode by in splendor.

*Mary Hall Swain was named Marietta High School principal, the first woman principal in the city and county. She held the position 11 years, then directed the curriculum for Marietta City schools and in 1966 joined the Kennesaw Junior College faculty. She died in June 2000.

Mary Hall Swain

1950

*Kennestone Hospital opened in June. Built on Church Street north of downtown Marietta, the facility has had many additions and renovations. During its 59 years, almost 200,000 babies have been delivered at the hospital. In 1988 the facility became known as WellStar Kennestone Hospital.

Ken Dickerson (right) the first baby born in Kennestone, June 13, 1950. Photo made July 1996.

*West Side and Lemon Street Elementary Schools were constructed. West Side building costs were $492,500, and $441,500 was spent for the Lemon Street construction. The Lemon Street building is now the Hattie Wilson Library.

*Varner's Drive-In was a favorite hangout of Marietta High School students when

it opened in the early 1950s. After school and on weekends, teenagers were seen at the popular spot, first opened on Roswell Street where Town & Country Shopping Center is now located. "World famous hotdogs," chili and barbecue drew scores of young people in their chrome-heavy autos despite parents' warnings not to go east of "the Four Lane," now Cobb Parkway. The drive-in later relocated just west on Roswell Street at the present site of Burlington Coat Factory.

1951

*With the Korean conflict heating up, the Lockheed Aircraft Corporation was selected by the U.S. Air Force to reopen Air Force Plant 6, modifying and upgrading 120 of the B-29s flown during World War II. Lockheed persuaded Jimmie Carmichael to return to the Marietta plant as general manager of Lockheed's Georgia Division.

*The Marietta Women's Club was responsible for the first arts organization in the city, the Fine Arts Club of Marietta. In 1983, the group became the Marietta-Cobb Fine Arts Center, and six years later, the Marietta/Cobb Museum of Art was created. The highly acclaimed museum is located at 30 Atlanta Street, originally the Marietta Post Office.

1953

*Marietta in the 1950s had a small town atmosphere embodied by the historic Cobb County courthouse, small locally owned businesses and large hardwood trees shading Glover Park. The town's population was 20,687.

*Lockheed Elementary School was built at a cost of $415,360. The facility now houses the Marietta School System's central office.

1955

*Banberry Elementary School opened. The school closed and the property was sold in 1987.

1956

*C.W. Bramblett was elected and served as mayor until 1959.

Bramblett (R) being sworn in on January 2.

1957

*Former Marietta resident and actress Joanne Woodward received an Oscar for her role in "Three Faces of Eve." The actress told city officials that attending movies at the Strand Theater during her childhood was one of the major reasons she became an actress.

Joanne Woodward

1958

*Sam J. Welsch was again named mayor.

*The first published color aerial photo of the Marietta Square was made by Joe McTyre as a test for a new color negative film released by Eastman Kodak.

1959

*Hickory Hills Elementary School in west Marietta was built at a cost of $550,000.

1960

*Marietta claimed a population of 25,500.

1961

*Southern Technical Institute (now Southern Polytechnic State University) held its first classes at the new Marietta campus on Clay Street (now South 120 Loop).

*Marietta-Cobb Area Vocational-Technical School received its charter.

*The U.S. Air Force awarded Lockheed a $1 billion contract for the C-141 Starlifter, the first military aircraft designed and built in Georgia.

*Lockheed took steps to complete racial integration of the work force.

*Bertie Lewis Blackman was the first black person to run for office in Marietta and Cobb County since the Reconstruction era. He qualified for Marietta's Ward 5 city council post but lost the election to pharmacist Howard "Red" Atherton.

1962

*Wright Street Elementary School opened. Construction cost was $284,200. Marietta Charter School is now located at the site.

*St. Joseph's Catholic Church School was the first school in Marietta and Cobb County to integrate classrooms.

*The famed Civil War locomotive "The General" again traveled through Marietta. The L&N Railroad sponsored the trip in observance of the 100th anniversary of the infamous Andrews Raid, a Yankee spy mission initiated in Marietta. The General began its centennial trip in Atlanta and continued to Chattanooga where it remained a captive until several court suits forced its return to Cobb County.

*Two prominent Mariettans, Mrs. Elizabeth Anderson Blair and Mrs. James R. Cowan, were among 62 Georgians killed in the crash of an Air France charter aircraft on June 2 in Paris.

1963

*S. R. "Tubby" Davis built Marietta's most famous landmark, the Big Chicken, on North Cobb Parkway. The original 56-foot-high eyecatching bird was designed to publicize Davis' fried chicken restaurant, the Chick, Chuck and Shake. The building, now the location of a Kentucky Fried Chicken Restaurant, has been completely restored. As the city's most prominent landmark, the Big Chicken guides lost motorists to their destinations and is a marker for pilots approaching Atlanta and nearby Dobbins Air Reserve Base.

*A 44.9 acre Cobb County-owned tract of land on Clay Street was sold for $233,000 in May.

*The State Supreme Court ruled that Marietta Mayor Sam Welsch had no legal right to hold the positions of mayor and city manager simultaneously.
* Several attempts by black citizens to desegregate downtown Marietta lunch counters proved unsuccessful.

*The new Marietta Post Office building opened on Lawrence Street. Construction cost was $350,000. The five digit ZIP codes began in January.

*A 300-pound safe containing narcotics was stolen from Atherton's Drug Company on the square.

*Cobb County government officials agreed to renovate the former post office building on Atlanta Street for use by the Cobb-Marietta Public Library.

*A huge explosion caused by a natural gas leak rocked the downtown area on Halloween night, killing seven people and injuring 23 others. The blast destroyed Atherton's Drug Company and left debris piled on the square.

*L.H. "Red" Atherton Jr. was elected mayor and served through 1969.

L.H. 'Red' Atherton Jr.

1964

*The first black students entered Marietta High School.

1965

*Lockheed won a $1.36 billion government contract to build the first 58 C-5 aircraft.

*Native Mariettan Billy Joe Royal's song, "Down in the Boondocks," was a hit, reaching Number 6 on the Cash Box magazine chart and Number 9 on the Billboard Hot 100 chart.

1967

*Marietta High School became fully integrated.

1968

*Spurred by business owner Bill Dunaway and the Marietta Jaycees, Marietta's traditional July 4 celebration was launched with a parade and other events.

1970

*James Richard Hunter was elected to a four-year term as mayor.

James Richard Hunter

1971

*Marietta Junior High School opened on Aviation Road. Built at a cost of $645,400, the school now houses the Marietta Sixth Grade Academy.

*In July, Marion Thomas, the first black member of the Marietta Housing Authority, was sworn in for a five-year term.

1972

*"The General," Civil War-era locomotive used by the Confederate Army, returned to Marietta on the way to its permanent home in Kennesaw. Crowds turned out along the route to see the famous engine.

1973

*Marietta's office of the National Association for the Advancement of Colored People (NAACP) opened. The organization is a strong civic force in the community.

*Deane Bonner,
President Cobb Branch, NAACP*

1974

*Marietta's railway freight depot built in the late 1800s was severely damaged in May when 11 boxcars of an L&N train jumped the tracks, plunged into the air and crashed into the building. An auto parts business also underwent heavy damage. The state demolished the depot rather than repairing the building.

*J. Dana Eastham was elected to two terms as mayor.

J. Dana Eastham

*Life University was chartered in Marietta. The chiropractic teaching institution now has an enrollment of 1,200 students.

1976

*The Downtown Marietta Development Authority (DMDA) was established with emphasis on redevelopment of the downtown business district. Phil McLemore was named director.

1977

*In a runoff election in October, Hugh Grogan won a seat on the Marietta City Council with 56 percent of the vote, becoming the first black person elected a city official. Grogan died in July 2009.

Hugh Grogan

*The final section of Interstate 75 in Georgia was completed four miles north of Marietta.

1978

*Atherton Square, a brick-paved area fronting the Marietta Welcome Center, was dedicated in memory of former Mayor Howard "Red" Atherton. Georgia Governor George Busbee attended the ceremonies.

1979

*Marietta's new City Hall on Lawrence Street was dedicated during Dana Eastham's term as mayor. Jack Crane was city manager. The city's contract with C. W. Matthews Construction Company for the building and parking deck was about $2.2 million.

1980

*Philip Goldstein was the youngest person elected to the Marietta City Council for the first of at least eight terms as Ward 7 representative. An attorney, he is the longest serving elected official in Marietta, has served as a Cobb assistant solicitor and manages his family's business interests.

Philip Goldstein

1982

*Theatre in the Square opened in the former railroad depot in downtown Marietta. The live theater production company, founded by Palmer Wells and the late Michael Horne, has received numerous awards and acclaim from its patrons. Its present location is on Whitlock Avenue near the square.

*Robert E. Flournoy Jr. was elected mayor. In 1987, he was appointed to a Cobb County Superior Court judgeship by Georgia Governor Joe Frank Harris and served until his death in 2003.

Robert E. Flournoy Jr.

*Marietta High School's expanded Winn Street campus was dedicated in December.

1984

*Spurred by a significant contribution from developer John Williams, Marietta carried out a major renovation of Glover Park with other funding from individuals and the city. The total project cost was approximately $2.5 million including $1 million from Williams. A new bandstand, gazebo, restored fountain, new shade trees,

landscaping, playground and other improvements were part of the restoration.

*The Marietta Welcome Center was created as part of the Marietta Sesquicentennial celebration. Theresa Jenkins was hired as executive director, a position she still holds today. The Welcome Center's first home was the former St. Joseph Catholic Church on Church Street razed in the late 1980s to make way for construction of the North 120 Loop.

1985

*The Marietta Welcome Center moved its office to the 1898 Western & Atlantic railway passenger depot near the railroad tracks on the west side of the square. The Welcome Center has received many awards and honors.

MWC Executive Director Theresa Jenkins (left) and staff.

1986

*Marietta's 50th mayor and first woman mayor, Victoria Franklin Chastain, was elected. A Marietta native, she previously served two terms as a city councilwoman.

Victoria Franklin Chastain

1987

*The Marietta Pilgrimage Christmas Home Tour made its inaugural appearance. Held the first weekend in December, it spotlights Marietta's historic homes and heritage public buildings. The Tour has been selected as a Top Twenty Event in the Southeast and a Top 100 Event in North America.

1988

*A. L. Burruss Elementary School was constructed, costing almost $4.6 million.

1990

*Longtime Cobb County Representative Joe Mack Wilson was elected mayor. He served until his death in May 1993.

Joe Mack Wilson

*Cobb Landmarks and Historical Society acquired the historic Root House, originally built on Church Street and later moved to Lemon Street. Business owner Bill Bullard donated the house to the organization and plans to move and restore the building went into operation. The city gave Cobb Landmarks permission to move the structure to a city-owned parcel at the 120 Loop and Lemon Street.

*Cobb County's new Central Library building, built at a cost of almost $7 million, opened on Roswell Street.

*Marietta's population reached 45,475.

1991
*City Club Marietta, an 18-hole public golf course on Powder Springs Street, opened after the former Marietta Country Club property was acquired and extensively renovated by the city. The original nine-hole layout was designed by Marietta Country Club members and constructed on the former site of the Georgia Military Institute.

1992
*The 1916 steam locomotive, manufactured by Glover Machine Works, was restored and put on display beside the railroad tracks across from Marietta Welcome Center and Visitors Bureau. The exhibit was dedicated on June 24.

*Marietta Fire Department shows off the restored "Aurora" fire engine in front of their headquarters. June 3, 1992.

*Flournoy Park, a city pocket park adjacent to the Cobb County Judicial Complex, honors Robert E. Flournoy Jr. Cobb County Commission Chairman Philip Secrist and Marietta Mayor Joe Mack Wilson participated in the

ceremony honoring the former Marietta mayor (1982-1986) and Cobb Superior Court judge (1987-2003).

*Joseph E. Brown Park, located next to the Confederate Cemetery, was named for the former Georgia governor. The park features the old Glover Park gazebo and flags representing all the Confederate states.

Joseph Emerson Brown

1993

*Ansley Little Meaders was elected to fill Joe Mack Wilson's unexpired mayoral term and also to two subsequent full terms.

Ansley Little Meaders

*Dunleith Elementary School was built. Building cost was about $6.5 million.

* "Marietta, Our Hometown," a video produced by the Marietta Welcome Center and Visitors Bureau and narrated by hometown girl, actress Joanne Woodward, debuted.

*Storm damage left a naked Big Chicken on New Years Eve. Property owners questioned the possibility of re-building but a huge outpouring of support caused KFC officials to approve a makeover for the Marietta landmark. Even though replacing the sheet metal bird cost roughly 20 times the cost of most KFC signs, company officials decided to spend as much as $200,000 to rebuild the Big Chicken. "We don't have anything like the Big Chicken anywhere in the world," a spokesman said.

1995

*The Marietta Museum of History opened its doors in the Kennesaw House. Under the leadership of Dan Cox, numerous excellent exhibits have been developed making the museum a big Marietta attraction.

*James "Friday" Richards was named Marietta High School's head football coach. He was the first African-American to be hired as head coach.

James "Friday" Richards

1996

*City Council members approved a $17.5 million 20-year bond for construction of a new Public Safety Complex.

*The city-owned Marietta Conference Center and Resort opened for business. Summer Olympics visitors to Atlanta helped fill the hotel during its first summer of operation. It is now known as the Hilton Atlanta/Marietta Hotel and Conference Center.

*The Root House Museum opened to the public with enthusiastic groups of students and adults enjoying tours led by authentically costumed docents. Marietta's first pharmacist, William Root, built the house about 1845.

*Cobb County's fifth Courthouse is located at the southeast intersection of Park Square and Washington Avenue.

1997

*Dan Cox of the Marietta History Museum holds old drugstore bottles found during sidewalk construction on Mill Street. They are from the William Root Drug Company in the 1870s.

1998

*A new Public Safety complex including, headquarters for police and fire departments, opened on July 11. Total cost of the project was $17.5 million.

2000

*Lee Rhyant became the executive general manager of Lockheed Martin plant in Marietta.

Lee Rhyant

*Marietta High School graduate Alan Ball received an Oscar for best screenplay for the movie "American Beauty." In 2002, Ball also won an Emmy for best directing for HBO's "Six Feet Under."

Alan Ball

*Marietta's population reached 58,748.

2001

*A new Marietta High School campus was completed on Whitlock Avenue at a cost of $58 million.

*Present enrollment of Marietta City Schools is approximately 7,600.

2002

*The city of Marietta was named one of ten Georgia "Cities of Excellence," recognized as one of the state's "best managed and most livable cities." A 12-member panel selected Marietta, grading on citizen participation, cultural arts, education and other categories.

*William B. Dunaway was elected Marietta's 53rd mayor. Dunaway, a longtime Marietta resident and Marietta High School graduate, is the former owner of Dunaway Drug Stores and the 1848 House restaurant, originally the plantation home of the town's first mayor, John Heyward Glover.

William B. Dunaway

2003

*The Gone With the Wind Museum: Scarlett on the Square opened featuring the collection owned by Dr. Chris Sullivan. The exhibit includes the only known original gown worn by Vivien Leigh in her role as Scarlett O'Hara. The museum is housed in the c. 1875 Thomas Building, formerly a cotton warehouse, carriage house and foundry.

(Left)
Vivien Leigh being fitted with the dress during the making of Gone With The Wind.

*Former Lockheed Georgia president Robert B. Ormsby founded the Marietta Aeronautical Museum and Education Center (later the Aviation Museum and Discovery Center). Cobb County acquired 15 acres near the corner of South Cobb

Drive and Atlanta Road from the U.S. Government, which the county subleased to the museum. By 2009, a Lockheed-built JetStar and C-141 Starlifter and four aircraft on loan from the U.S. Navy were moved to the museum site.

2005

*Marietta City Council members taking the oath of office in 2005 are (L to R): Annette Lewis, Ward 1; Grif Chalfant, Ward 2; Holly Walquist, Ward 3; Van Pearlberg, Ward 4; Anthony Coleman, Ward 5; Jim King, Ward 6; and Philip Goldstein, Ward 7. Georgia Court of Appeals Judge Debra Bernes conducted the ceremony.

*The Marietta City Council approved a historic preservation ordinance and appointed the first Historic Preservation Commission. Ray Worden served as the first commission chair.

*Sawyer Road Elementary School opened. Construction cost amounted to $14 million.

*The City Council committed $5 million to purchase rental properties plagued by crime and neglect. In November, city officials broke ground on a $55 million mixed use redevelopment in the heart of the city. The Manget Street project includes owner-occupied single-family detached homes, attached

single-family town houses and residential condominium buildings.

2006

Marietta

★★★★★
All-America City

2006

*Marietta was selected one of the ten best communities in the nation as a 2006 All-America City, the oldest and most respected community recognition award in the country. It was the first time in 30 years that a Georgia city won. The city's selection as a winner substantiated the community as a national model with extensive planning efforts and approaches to facing difficult challenges in innovative and collaborative ways. Marietta demonstrated how three unique projects are working through community partnerships. These include: efforts to reduce crime and stabilize deteriorating neighborhoods through M-STAR, a citywide program combining community policing and computer analysis of crime trends; a Revitalization Program aimed at preventing decline of neighborhoods and increasing the percentage of homeowners; and Marietta Reads, a citywide effort through the Marietta City Schools to foster reading and literacy.

*Marietta Power and Water celebrated the 100th anniversary of its founding.

2007

*The city launched Project MINT (Marietta Initiative for Neighborhood Transformation) with construction of a new house for a low-to-moderate income family. In partnership with Cobb Housing Inc. (CHI), older homes needing repairs are purchased and rehabilitated or rebuilt, then sold to other families for home ownership.

*William B. Dunaway was reelected mayor. He continued to work on fulfilling his campaign goals.

2008

*Marietta City Council and the Board of Lights and Water approved a $405 million investment over the next 40 years for an expansion of Plant Vogtle nuclear plant that will allow the city to have cleaner energy and base power for decades to come. The city will own 64 megawatts of power each year that will be generated by the new reactors.

*Meeting Park, a new mixed-used development, opened on the former site of Marietta Housing Authority's Clay Homes on Roswell Street near the Marietta Square.

*The Historic Marietta Trolley Company made its debut with popular tours of the downtown square, antebellum houses and Kennesaw Mountain battlefields. The Trolley departs from 131 Church Street each day except Monday.

2009

*The grand opening of the restored Strand Theater, an art deco movie house built in 1935 on North Park Square, was held January 9. Renamed the Earl Smith Strand Theater, the $4.1 million restoration was led by Friends of the Strand, a non-profit group of business and community representatives. Public and private donations financed the project. The Strand offers live theater performances, concerts, classic movies, and is available for weddings, receptions and parties.

*Ground breaking was held for Cobb County's sixth courthouse in Marietta in May. The new building will occupy the corner of Lawrence and Haynes streets and is expected to be completed in 2010.

*Marietta serves as the setting for the annual Juneteenth, a celebration of the date the last slaves in America were freed. Hundreds gathered in Glover Park for food, games, music and other entertainment sponsored by the NAACP's Cobb County branch.

*The Marietta Fire Department gives tours throughout the year. Children visited the main fire station on Haynes Street.

*Marietta began a huge project to improve streetscape and road corridors. Projects already completed are planting more than 500 trees, sidewalk upgrades and beautification efforts including decorative street lamps and landscaped medians.

*The Marietta Historic Preservation Commission approved a proposal to designate three city-owned properties as historic landmarks: the Clarke Library building on Church Street, Brumby Hall on Powder Springs Street and the city waterworks building on Sessions Street.

Above clockwise; Clarke Library, Brumby Hall and Marietta Waterworks Building on Sessions Street.

*Like previous generations, Marietta residents flock to the Farmers Market held on Saturdays on North Park Square. As many as 1,000 customers visit the market's 60 vendors from May until December to buy fresh produce, flowers, homemade jams, jellies, honey, pastries and organic dog biscuits.

*A Memorial Wall inscribed with names of Confederate soldiers buried in the Confederate Cemetery and ten unique Civil War-related sculptures are a new feature of Joseph E. Brown Park and the Cemetery. The park's refurbishing is funded by the Confederate Cemetery Foundation and Friends of Brown Park.

*The city's population is approximately 67,562. Marietta is the tenth largest city in Georgia.

*A neighborhood party, ribbon cutting and plaque unveiling were part of the city's celebration of the reopening of Henry Memorial Park at Reynolds and Wright streets. The park was established in 1954, a gift to the community by Willie Louise Henry Burford in memory of her parents, John and Peggy Henry.

*The City of Marietta kicked off its yearlong 175th anniversary January 14 by unveiling the anniversary logo and web site and launching a year of events that included neighborhood parties, festivals, parades and events in downtown Glover Park. Volunteers formed seven subcommittees representing the Marietta community, including business, culture, education, government, history, neighborhood/civic and religious groups that meet throughout the year to plan events and activities to celebrate Marietta's past, present and future.

Old Marietta Post Cards
Courtesy of Bob Basford Collection

Mills McNeel house, built c. 1895 on Church Street.

Marietta Square, c. 1890s

Senator A. S. Clay's home on Atlanta Street.

Stereo card of the Kennesaw House.

South Park Square early 1920s.

Brumby Recreation Center with the first public swimming pool in Marietta.